CROSSROADS OF DREAMS

Crossroads of Dreams

A Poetry Anthology

Franklin Agogho
Jude A. Fonchenalla
M.D. Mbutoh

Spears Media Press
Denver, Colorado

Spears Media Press LLC
Denver
7830 W. Alameda Ave, Suite 103-247 Denver, CO 80226
United States of America

First Published in 2020 by Spears Media Press
www.spearsmedia.com
info@spearsmedia.com
Information on this title: www.spearsmedia.com/crossroads-of-dreams

ISBN: 9781942876519 (Paperback)

Also available in Kindle (eBook)

Cover design by Doh Kambem
Text design and typesetting by Spears Media Press LLC, Denver, CO

Dedicated to Cameroonian and African youths all over the world. We pray that the words herein speak to you and shape your vision for a new world.

Contents

FOREWORD

Beyond being an "anthology" *stricto sensu*, *Crossroads of Dreams* is a veritable specimen of poetic collaboration. By its sustained and congenial thematic resonances, it is a close-knit transmission of kindred poetic heartbeats. In literary history, poetic collaboration has often constituted a major hallmark of creative yearning and literary attainment. If we take the English context, for instance, Lord Alfred Tennyson and Arthur Hallam planned to publish a joint collection as a seal of their friendship before the latter prematurely died, converting the dreamt-for and unrealized collaboration into a subject of unrivalled poetic inspiration for Tennyson. The trio of the Brontë sisters, i.e., Charlotte, Emily and Anne launched their literary careers in the mid 19th century through a joint collection of *Poems* under the respective pennames of Currer, Ellis and Acton Bell that signalled the blossoming of a brilliant literary career, even though Anne's genius was only acknowledged posthumously. In the present collection, we are privy to the strident echoes of three young Cameroonian poets, each with his (s)pace, rhythm and sensibility but all of whom are undeniably endowed with talent and visions of resilience against a dissonant and disconcerting present characterized by social decay and political infamy. With these three voices, there is a heterophonic and centrifugal synthesis of Dynosian insurrection, crystalline Apollonian vision as well as serene allegorical wisdom. The result is a synchrony of soul(mate)s that enhance social communication and creative extraversion, deconstructing the normative perception of poetry as a solitary, solipsistic, cryptic and even esoteric enterprise.

In terms of subject matter, the poems contained in this volume are varied. However, certain aspects seem to be recurrent and central. As a matter of fact, most of the poems relate to youth and youthfulness both as a locus of enunciation and as a thematic focus, decrying a socio-political dispensation that has led to immobilism as a result of gerontocratic (mis)governance. In a context where youths are represented in clichéd slogans as "leaders of tomorrow" and "spearhead" of the nation, the poetic voices call for a reconsideration of deviant youth culture in order to unleash the creative forces of personal and collective redemption. The youths purported to be the determinants of African future are the same who escape economic malaise in pursuit of the mirage of European/American green pastures with its attendant ordeals and tragedies: "For brothers roaming the fruitful streets of motherland/ Loading lost bags on the sweat of family's weak reserve/For a death walk to ruins in the heart of sandy wilderness... Ancestors weep to eulogy - borne planes/Flying in sons lost to lunacy/Who escaped their fatherland of streets full of plenty/ Ravished by the few, by the savvy ("Zion: Home" by F. Agogho).

While the quest for human dignity is a human right, the poets frown at unfounded and unrealistic aspirations for material possession and ostentatious lifestyle that have instilled a culture of suicidal risk amongst African youths. Several of the poems address the prevalence of what Joseph Tonda in his Impérialismes Postcoloniales (Postcolonial Imperialisms, 2015) refers to as a culture of fascination with luxury and glitz which has underlined African history from the slave trade to postcolonial society: "We have lost us, in the culture/While bargaining to be them in their subcultures/Of fashion, disrespect and misdemeanours/Their lives shaping our lives/And their colour and wigs becoming our preferences" ("Amongst us", by J.A. Fonchenella). Such poems, in line with what Tonda defines as the culture of bedazzlement (éblouissement), subvert the pursuit of superficial surfaces and misleading illusions in the face of more urgent socio-political projects that require youthful energy and perspectives.

In a context of postcolonial realpolitik where venal expediency, sloganeering and conformism have become the order of the day while ethically conscious citizens are perceived as social outcasts due to a general reversal of values, the poets feel the urgency to express their visions and dreams in synergy. In his insightful text, *Les Jeunes et l'Ordre Politique en Afrique postcolonial* (*Youth and Political Order in Postcolonial Africa*, 1985), Mbembe underscores the intricate effects of political degeneration under the one-party regimes, delineating new forms of expressions and modes of survival amongst the youths that emerged from such dispensations. In what he characterizes as esophageal politics whereby the state relates with the citizenry primarily in the form of rhetoric and feasting, the youths become vectors of prebendal politics in the service of the old order. If his analysis focuses on the one-party systems prior to the wind of democratization, the poetic reflections contained in this volume dissect youthful habits and dilemmas in a pseudo-democratic dispensation. However, in spite of the difference in temporality, the principles and practices of state depletion and youthful delinquency remain identical: "These youth are the dregs of the palm wine that /Lingers beneath cups of old greedy constipation ("Listen to Them", M.D. Mbutoh). The habitus inculcated by these youths augurs a grim picture of the future, hence the urgency for a fundamental change of mentalities and a re-ordering of priorities. In the aforementioned book, Mbembe poses the challenge facing the postcolonial society with regard to the youths in the following terms: Through what mechanisms should we integrate in our society a percentage of our population that is always on the rise and in the quest of a new social dynamism? How do we avoid the underutilisation of youthful capacities and energies? How do we ensure that they play an important role in important social and political configurations of our society? (1985 :243).

In such a context, the poet poses as the moral conscience of the society and is disposed to point out, like Plato's philosopher, that the realities pursued with much frenzy are mere shadows. This perhaps accounts for the commingling of images of glitz and glare with ubiquitous description of the underworld, the lower scrotum characterised by faeces, sweat, urine and waste in most of the poems by all the three collaborators. Through faecal imagery, euphonious political discourses are consistently interpolated with depictions of a disfiguring reality, subverting the primacy of speech that has taken the place of actual action in the postcolony. Given the silver line(n)s that lace the poems, we are bound to interpret these faecal imageries through a Bakhtinian lens wherein scatological images are equivocal in creative works with carnivalesque tonality, as are most of the poems in the volume: "The images of faeces and urine are ambivalent, as are all the images of the material bodily lower stratum; they debase, they destroy, regenerate, and renew simultaneously. They are blessing and humiliation at the same time" (Rabelais and his World, 1983:151). The scatological images therefore represent the ambivalent relation between the reality of decay and the possibility of the germination of something new.

In the entire collection, there is an unmistakable Promethean quest for the dismantling of the old order, which is also the order of the old, so as to make way for a new dawn that would lead to the reconstitution of individual bodies and collective dreams. It should be noted that the old are not wholly characterized as undesirable and despicable in the entire collection. When a life has been lived according to ethical principles and in defence of the collective good, it deserves celebration as an inspiration to the younger generation. One of the poets captures this perception quite succinctly: "On her back lay the trace of weight/Imposed relentless by life, the sure race/To feed the young, mould the weak/And assure the brave that life is not to take with greed" ("Age is Gold", by F. Agogho). However, given the rarity of such responsible adulthood, especially in the political sphere, there is a strong sense of discontent with the old who have, in their excessive greed for power, enlisted the youth into an unproductive commensalic rapport with the state. Thus, the old are viewed as an obstruction to cosmic harmony: "Longevity of old carcasses above gravestones/Only starve the maggots" ("Is it all Lost?", by M. D. Mbutoh). To borrow from Harold Bloom's concept of the anxiety of influence, this collection can be considered as the askesis (self-purgation) of the ephebes (the young poets), in their determination to assert their presence in and affirm their visions of the world against the stifling influence of avaricious precursors and a cannibalistic system of national and global governance.

Dr. Gilbert Shang Ndi
Romance Studies/Comparative Literature
University of Bayreuth, Germany

I
(IR)RESPONSIBILITY, DESPAIR & FRUSTRATION

Cliques

Roses aren't meant for lean fabrics,
Woven in the backyards of blacksmiths
Who hammer on the efforts of meritocracy,
Shattering dream petals on platforms of reverend lunacy.

He said in his youth,
He will break banks and wreck ruin.
He said in his youth,
He will sell tomorrow to taste truth.

And so truth dances in the parlours of interest,
Twirling on the hinds of patience,
Drinking to the ranks of influence,
Laying drunk on the shoulders of clique sergeants.

Cliques of tailored indifference,
Built on the mockery of titled goons
Who cook easy soups on affluence,
Drawing home famished youths to bloody tables.

It is a clique world
With dense jungles of soul-searching buffoons,
Stoned on ravenous tales of lack,
Who sell their souls before they get them back.

FRANKLIN AGOGHO

High

I'm high on a thought,
a thought that I've sought,
The thought that there is a thought,
Which, in first place, I shouldn't have thought.

I'm high, yeah I'm high,
That the thought has led me to a style
Of life, it looks like I'm high,
On shit coming from her mind.

I'm high like swine on feed,
Like a Jah Man on weed.
But anguish is my weed,
Solitude, my spot of peace.

I'm high on the words,
Hovering in my mind like a cloud of dust.
I'm high on the phrase,
'It's over, but don't take it like a serious case.'

FRANKLIN AGOGHO

I Cut my Hair

I sought to spark a flame,
To exhibit my pain.
I sought to scream at the lame dames,
To show my frustration in glowing to fame.
I sought to bark my hunger like a hungry dog,
To lure my master back to my pot.
I sought to scream and spit,
Like a preacher preaching at the pulpit.
I sought the voice that speaks
Relief and riches.
I sought to rip off my skin,
And expose the wound eating deep within.

A sting stung at my song early before chorus,
Relegating my verse of sighs to a note of naught.
Essence in my days sweep away like dirt under a broom,
I seek a hammer to break to respite walls erected against my
quintessence.

Mother cried me not to fade
In hopeless hope hovering around my dreams like a dark block-
ade.
A strong desire for eminence, affluence and affection drowns
me,
Deep like a lone lamp in a dark forest, thick.

A voice whispers impetus,
But it whispers too low.
So I cut my hair to bare my troubles,
And sing my eulogy before am gone.

FRANKLIN AGOGHO

3

Monumental Deceit

I love me,
I know I love me,
But,
Times make me hate me,
Not for much love for me,
Not because living life is shit,
It was just monumental deceit.
I saw it,
Lived it,
Ate it,
Wished it,
Was sure of it,
Got close,
So close to love it,
But again,
It was deceit.
Sometimes I hate my soul,
Because even when rubbing shoulders with divinity,
It fails to give me proximity,
To reality.

REALITY!

Monumental deceit.

FRANKLIN AGOGHO

4

Paranoia

A string of light cuts through my darkness,
It seems to wipe out my sadness,
Memories get lost in excess,
Everything feels right, relentless.

She's here,
She's mine,
She's everything and nothing I fear,
They were all lies.

I remember,
We met on the bus.
Dating, we cruised to Kimbo,
Then, ate like squirrels in a love dance,
And made love, plenty, it wasn't once.

Liars!
You did not see,
Did not see when it started,
When it started it was me and her,
And her love was like the shadow of the sun on a beautiful morning.

No!
Let us be.
Insanity is not me,
I'm sane, I implore thee.
She's smiling at me, can't you see?

Release me, haters.
How can you say she's betrothed?
To another, it's madness.
I'll slay, if I must, to prove my innocence.

It's thanks to you,
Darkness returns,
Chewing away the light that spiced my being,
The shadow of my shadow hangs over my shadow.

I open my eyes,
Blood litters on all my sides,
A knife; I'm numb on both wrists,
Then I fall into a deep sleep.

FRANKLIN AGOGHO

The Gutter

Down, down the street in Korupt Ville,
Amidst cars buzzing and souls hurrying,
Tight collars and fashion-torn jeans hustling,
A stench seizes the air,
A terrible reek,
The gutter's scent.

Pressed nostrils hurry by
Avoiding rottenness expressing itself.
In wonders, eyes and brains wonder why
The stench is so harsh and vile.

In the algae mature gutter,
Used rubber floats in honourable display.
Shit, in lumps, dance with alcoholic assonance,
Some drunkard slept in there yesterday.

In there,
There is an exhibition,
Of credentials destined for employ,
Pay slips of cheats cashed by bribed cashiers,
Lotto tickets sinking in lost despair,
And state contracts greased by cheap puff balls.

A Mad Man pisses in total indifference,
A lady bends too, no public shame,
Affluence, from a limousine, dumps barely squeezed citrus,
Some street kid jumps in to redeem what he can eat.

The gutter is blocked desperately,
So desperately, its unknown chemical insides can't go by,
Keeping its staggering stench in place,
And everybody walks alright.

Then,
A crowd gathers,
There is an infant cry.
Somebody dumped their offspring, no morose.
Pity crowds the populace,
But all fear to pull the poor soul out.

I stare in awe
As a dog drinks from this stench filled gutter,
And as I aim to rescue offspring from contemporary decay,
The beast leaps forward
And bites me deep into my insides,
Corrupting me incorrigibly.

That's how corruption stole my soul,
Cos' I strove to save a poor soul,
Stuck in the stench filled gutter.

FRANKLIN AGOGHO

The Stranger's Cry

I heard the stranger cry,
Her sobs deep like the echoes from a wailing soul in a dark
trench.
I heard the stranger laugh,
Like disbelieve was flirting on her mind's mesh.

Under the compound tree, in the blue hospital, patients stream-
ing in spree,
I heard them talk on the phone,
'Mama is gone, she is no more slow,'
She sleeps.

The pain strikes my heart like their weed was mine,
Which I had to smoke to stupor today,
A weed they sought to blot out that day,
Though tomorrow was going to hurt again.

'O my God, O my God,' their echoing wails drool
'Why did you take her? She was a kind soul'
They wail again, in coordinated tunes,
Profane their hurts, cook it like stew.

A tear tickles my eye lids,
Recording the vision of pale souls, grim faces, on sick beds,
Bound to hear wails, mourning souls past,
Pity meets my sorrow, pushing my tears back.

I rise to leave, flee the deep wails,
But see a nurse grin, her job done, she is on the phone,
« Bonjour chérie, tu me manques, ça va? »
And I wonder who, under this tree, is gonna write a poem when
chérie's time comes.

FRANKLIN AGOGHO

What If

What if heaven smiled on me?
Brushing away my stagnant skin,
Powdering to handsomeness, a smile released,
Will this hostility decease?

What if my name rang sweet in enterprise?
Stirring trade to run my way, no surprise,
Coaxing cash to dash alongside,
Will the mind get back on the ride?

What if captivity evaded depravity?
Bringing family to sanity,
Cocktailing a future that shines with meritocracy,
Will I be rewarded for my imperturbability?

What if the wheel of time spun a while back?
Inviting attitude generous in attack,
Slapping me into a fool, for no reason on my back,
Will I get regret due, with no relax?

What if I held the magic wand in this senseless strive?
To exalt the world, like I've done throughout time,
Helping the earth, even when there's none to provide,
Will I still bless when all smiles decide to hide?

What if...? What if...?

Franklin Agogho

10

Always

Lately, I have received a lot of word of hate.
Dad says I am not eighteen, but twenty-eight.
And that my friends were young and not my age mates.
He always complimented me as Mr Late.
I couldn't understand him, though I felt his rage.

It was the tenth night and I needed the television.
Destined to change my destiny, I carved a vision,
And waited on the bosses' speech to state the mission.
And although we had consumed much of his illusions,
We were still amazed with the cuteness of fake dictions.

The hour came and we all were inferred,
Urged, to consider agriculture and never to defer.
I was ready and trusted no other activity could interfere,
So I got a land and to the land code I was referred.
That was when I realised the constitution was unfair.

I was told that legally I couldn't own the land
Not the addressed youth or anyone of my band
Deceived – what really was mine was the sand
My head couldn't save me, not even my hands
I went back to my room changing the radio band

What am I supposed to do to guard my future,
When misery, no hope, and deceits are found in one mixture?
Am I supposed to forge or wait my turn on the fixture?
Youths forced to live lives void of credited texture.
While munching hates, plights pressure is pleasured by nature.

JUDE A. FONCHENALLA

11

Front and Back Wheels

We aren't locomotives
Or their rolls,
So why expect me to game like I was cramped
On a railing?
The reason why I am not my father;
And my brothers aren't him too,
And I'm not my brothers.
And none of them wants to be me
But we remain us.
So I ask;
Why do you ignore my certificates
To ask me who Dad was?
Seriously, I didn't attend the same school
With my Dad
So we share no common experience.
Probably,
Sadi did because his Dad was a youth
When his mates retired.
Anyway I share destiny with none
And that's the reason I strived not to be Dad.
He put in his best
So that my brothers and I wouldn't be him –
He dreamt to be the last gardener
In the lineage and to see Offspring of his
Differ from low calls.
You caged me, not with barbed wires
But with the illicit thought
That accident is assured
When the back wheels
Take over the front wheels,
Like we were locomotives and not humans.
And that is how you've judged
And sealed my fate

Not to rise above a gardener's.
Must I never be successful than Bello?
Because my Dad trimmed their flowers
And my uncles washed for his uncle?
Must I serve him?
When he dropped out of what I master?
His father was the front wheel in their time
And mine was the back,
So I'm fated to be the energy
That glows in him?
Why read my person from a dangling image
Of a mover
When you're eyeing at a still mirror
Projecting a candid double
Or are the mind's eye blinded at anything candid?
Well if I must play in your field,
The back wheels have always pushed the front
To give speed.
In life overtaking is allowed if deserved genuinely
So quit protein sequence bands.

Jude A. Fonchenalla

How Genuine

Sarcastic how they make geniuses
From half-baked brains.
Applauding them on realizations
Whose archives have no genesis.
Youths as tomorrow's leaders
Become a tag kept for those with ladders.
And famously they accept;
For absolute power corrupts absolutely.
That is the national legacy passed on
Carefully so it fits as inheritance
And they receive a meritocratic hat
On blood base to justify the old tag.

After hitting goals via chromosomes,
They identify with us as youths,
With hopes that our voices mix for their betterment.
Well, I saw water and oil blend with a whizzer
What's your anticipated outcome
Now that you wear the readymade crown?
Because you feel caught?
And in you we see a reflection,
A reflection that is all of them
And I hear the old adage resounding;
Fresh wine in the old jar taste the same like the old wine.
So they used you; part of us, to fight us.
Now we know it's a two-front thing –
The old hags clinching to power
While tagging us as leaders of a sold tomorrow
While they using genetics to elect who's fit amongst us.

JUDE A. FONCHENALLA

The Unfaithful Dance

'Hello! Are you there?
She wanted to know if he was actually there.
Not that she cared,
But not to be noticed was her fear.
No answer came to answer her call of dare
So she called again with a 'hello!'
And waited shadily on he who she fears will answer the hello.
None came, but grumbles.
Not noticing the moans because she trembled.
Not wanting to tear he who was drawing her fears.
Then the unwanted guest of consciousness tapped in,
And she sat to rethink and re-strategize should in case.
Again, she called 'Hello', this time with consciousness.
Drawing near, she clearly heard moments in haste
And for once she prayed it wasn't the case.
The cautions were marshy
As the whole act of betrayal proved nasty
She crawled with energy,
Searching frantically for the hat on her head.
Everyone in the hood, understood the synergy
But it was her first,
Dealing with swallowing her own pills of unfaithfulness –
Her companion hasting frantically into another ladylike.
Everyone striped, even her who escaped another wife
And his man was being taken for good.

JUDE A. FONCHENALLA

It's Dusk

The sun has been up for so long now,
Its bright eye has become too good for
Our soft skins and has rendered us bald and coarse.

We have watched the gaits of the sun
As it walked across the yard like the
Martyrs of freedom basking over the yard they gained.

The shadows grow from the manure the sun
Puts beneath their toes, and the fowls seek
Their beds, and the nda'a bird is up for a showdown.

The serpent basks beneath the spikes of the dead palms,
The lions and panthers file their claws to pacify the
Civil strife growing in their entrails,

It is dusk, sir! Oh! Is it?
It's been a long day— there can only be eight days
In the market week, no more, no less!

It's dusk, dear comrades of the tiger skin
And the warmness of your children's mother's enticement
Beckons you into the matrimonial bed of retirement.

Tomorrow shall be another day for the cube to
Wet its claws with the dews of yesternight's bath,
The night shall wash today's follies with its dews.

It's dusk dear husband and the children are in their
Hut, your porridge is cooked just the way you like it,
And, there is nothing under my loin, too!
Long you have been gone, and the forbears are in a
Council to overturn your chair of wisdom—
But before dusk closes its lids, what about une nuit, mon cher?

M.D. MBUTOH

Hollow Stems

They walk in multitudes of shapes of sizes,
Masked youthful faces with coats of affability.
These youth!

You would think these coats of smiles lie
On beds of beautiful spirits and fresh carcasses,
But this is a basket of deplorable!

Knocked together by old tales— like
The Roman populace ere the death of Caesar
Hollow ideas cramp their brains like Dangote's cement.

Hollow stems dancing in a precarious wind,
Toilet vapours spewed into tired nostrils
And eyes turned skyward like cursed Chinese ghosts!

They are hollow stems, these youth:
Filled with sags of octogenarian faeces from
Morn' to evening, cursed generation.

M.D. MBUTOH

Song of Frustration

Budding seeds and tassels
If you hear this song do not think
I am sad, for sadness has no room here!

Age is excrement, and we all are beetles
Snorting from no entry to no exit

Great bards and griots,
Do not think my heart is wrought in
The tiger snare—dust your legs!

Age is excrement, and we all are beetles
Snorting from no entry to no exit

I hear the song of prisoners in glass
Buildings chanting incessantly,
Fear not, for the tick shall fall off when intoxicated.

Age is excrement, and we all are beetles
Snorting from no entry to no exit

Youthfulness is a glinting diamond
In the earth's womb, and old age is
Mushroom—no room for polemics please!

Age is excrement, and we all are beetles
Snorting from no entry to no exit

Some of us may not know the
Sourness of unripe fruits, for there is
A medicine beneath the public tree,
Age is excrement, and we all are beetles
Snorting from no entry to no exit

But ignorance is no foolishness, and in wickedness
Lies frustration— a ghost at a crossroad, no
One to take it home for proper burial.

Age is excrement, and we all are beetles
Snorting from no entry to no exit

Hear this; we are in gestation, and this
Foetus must be born regardless of the whips
Of the red eye warder kept to cage ingenuity.

Age is excrement, and we all are beetles
Snorting from no entry to no exit

A river eventually finds its course
Down a valley—
But its entrails will sweep the dirty forest floor.

M.D. MBUTOH

The Staggerer

We heard your voice
Roaring through the midnight
Streets, beaten by a bottle!

Babes were terrified when your
Coarse symphony injected nightmares
In the peaceful mind of the sun's closed eyes.

Your shadow ghosted
Late night keepers like
Yourself—Beau-Fort impregnated you.

Your tongue was palatable and you
Rolled foreign languages like the Pentecost
Soldiers of Christ when tongues of fire descended.

Your sour scent, petrified head
Reeling like a frenzied tornado
In the fever of the harmattan drums.

I saw your image, like in the
Dreams of Jared Angira,
Wiggling and dwindling like dying flames.

Then, I saw you in the morning
Gliding on top speed, as if separating
From your shadow.

Your head hides in the coldness
Of the sky— you live with the giraffe, hardly
Conscious of the jiggers in the toes of your village!
You eat your own eggs like
The pig devours its piglets, and watch old

Masquerade juju your future down boulders.

I see the look of a humbled slave in you,
You toe the line like obedient cowries
On Kunta Kinte's chains, highway into the boat.

Broken sol eating and being eaten
By the teeth of the tar— a long-faced salvation is
Lost in the forest and pus is served for the people's lunch!

The standard is mediocrity, and competency
Is a debased form, scavengers don't live on
Cakes, so are they, the maggots!

M.D. MBUTOH

Conversation with Self

I counted the bottoms of the nails buried in the ceiling's flesh
Above me, noting every inch through the parallel lines
Betwixt the cheap plywood hastily glued on weevil-infested
Planks, maybe to hold rat droppings from adding to my bowl of
gari.

This half-interred shack has been my haven for the past
Octave and a dozen moons.
There was this time, this time when my itchy ears couldn't
Rest from the mournful touch of my woman neighbour's late
night ecstasies!

Ah, dear poor rich room and young weary bodies!
Soon the landlord would come with puppy ears dangling over
Gray hair, like a badly beaten women's used pad: a bundle of
tiercé papers
Taking refuge under the armpit of snuff-smeared suit, numbed
toes in—

"Makara naaa?"
"Ooweii!" I would answer.
That's how sweet the conversation would go if the tail of
The moon is still fifteen days away.

Then you tune an old television set, a really aged set winking like
A midnight monkey under the surprise torch of the hunter—
« Les jeunes d'aujourd'hui sont les leadeurs de demain »
An old tailed prime mate perches on a parliamentary anvil,

Hitting something so hard that looks like a sledge hammer
On a 1960 imported mahogany table— to drive his message into
The heads of doubting Odogos, Ndumbes, Tambes and Tatas.
Tomorrow belongs to the buds and today to brown leaves— aha!

M.D. Mbutoh

II
FAMILY, HUMANISM
&
LOVE

For Mother

The seed fell on thorny soil
In the King's backyard.
The seed fell on thorny soil
Cos' it dropped into the king's bag.

It rained drops, whips on her hind.
It hailed messy rain, scars on her strive.
From inception to germination,
The seed fell on thorny soil,
Peeling off her faint cotyledons in mocking laughter.

The seed fell, bearing judgment in the ridicule of her there.
The seed fell on thorny soil,
Germination fell in dupe to reason and despair.

The seed fell, and flowered at last,
Dodging hardship, thorns of temptation and rocks in blasts.
Flowery blossoms coloured the sphere of death,
The seed fell in birth but shone majesty within blurs.

Then it rose in strength,
Towering the palace and beautifying the slain rear.
The seed fell and grew on sand,
Though winds blew foundation, sinking her stand in sabotage.

But she throve and glowed,
With branches and fruit nursing seeds in juicy cones.
The seed fell from the words of the King,
Being His pride, his peace.

The seed was you, Is you,
True.

To mother, who glowed even when all slowed.

FRANKLIN AGOGHO

Steadfastness

On the road to the city of light,
Within nests caged in coconut hair,
Little birds tweet,
Blind tweets,
Hungry tweets,
For mother to quench their thirst.

Defenceless limbs in growing feathers cloaked in darkness,
Ignorant of the world's true gaze,
And mother's face,
Still tweet their hunger,
Certain that mother, even long, will surely feed their worm cravings.

Steadfastness.

FRANKLIN AGOGHO

We Were Once Ten

It was then when she kissed my cheek,
I played the game nature's way, not my purse, it was far away.
It was then when I forgot my nose,
Catarrh couldn't compete with friends' care, my growth.
It was then when home was our smiles,
Our blood had no face, no colour, a shelter to hide.
It was then when I ran to mama at first glance,
Evil hadn't domicile in a cage invaded by ignorance.
It was then when she danced in the splash,
Nude in showers with him,
No hair, no fear, no agitated itches,
Just flat chests, slayed complex, breathing like souls with no sex.

It was then when I ate, didn't care,
If she fed to resemble the white missionaries who lived with
The family who, on palm oil, ate breakfast with cocoyam
Because our uniforms shone same in the morning.

It was then when we needn't need ten tens to love,
Like rust engines clinging on oil to work.

It was then when we were once ten.
Can't today live eternal tens?

FRANKLIN AGOGHO

Listen to Them

Listen to them because they hardly
Listen to themselves—they lost it once and for all.

They do not know they have a voice made of gold
And a shining sword in the guise of tongue!

These youth are the dregs of the palm wine that
Lingers beneath cups of old greedy constipation.

Listen to them, for they have lost touch with reality—
Their very existence hovers in dark clouds over praying heads.

Youthfulness is the wood on which the ailing fire of old age
feeds,
But then no infested faggot is useful to any household!

So listen to them while the wax is still young on their ears,
For once beaten twisteth forever like a schooled ox.

But listen to these soldier ants while the wind is asleep,
A severed plantain stem is excrement that never decays.

M.D. Mʙᴜᴛᴏʜ

To Fonlon, that He May rest in Peace

Pardon the foolishness of a child who fails to ask
Why its forebear's exploits are never mentioned when title
Holders are hailed and graced with black caps and red feathers!

Pardon the selfishness of budding generation who hides itself
In the clouds of its own dreams chasing mirages into rough
boulders,
This, great scholar, we are guilty of and more...

We have wronged you beyond repairs, for it serves no purpose
Pouring libations over dead mount of red earth when the soul
duels in
The council of elders in their interminable grandeur.

We have waved your memory with left paws and basked in
The enemy's camp for too long and your grave is beginning
To gape its mouth like opened ulcer in the body of the earth.

We realise the gods have left us at a crossroad because we left
you
In your cave and never came back to pay you a visit!
Experience has humbled us down like fallen breasts and we have
failed!

Our cultural nakedness weeps with timidity when we sail across
White clouds into the house of he-that-the-gods-sent-to-kill-our-
memory!
We forget easily like brains that sit on kegs of the best raffia
wine.

We tell tall tales in the womb of the earth like bards in cold
deserts
When ears are mummified, and our suppressors drink wine in
The skulls of our buds and beat celebratory drums with our
femurs.

M.D. MBUTOH

III
GENDER, FEMINISM, THE GIRL CHILD

Breasts

Dual rounds of coconuts
Flow milk and water in fresh dots,
Sprinkling existence on stones and rocks
To wet sand, heal the land,
Though desert ruled like an angry god.

Risen chests beautify woman-kind
To share love, give life,
And suckle youth and adult through strive,
Even to mad masters who swoon
Cos' they all are babies and need her presence, her moon.

FRANKLIN AGOGHO

Mami Planti

A multi patched umbrella refuges her stead,
Casting an assuring shadow on a plump frame.
Sweat drizzles down her burnt skin,
Fertile from heat sailing in from live coal in the stove.
She writhes as she cajoles plantains to edibility,
But is accustomed to burns from roasting plums.
Halting is no option, her mission still in infancy,
Maturity still lives down in slums.
Her oddly casual allure doesn't deter her,
Nor perception which shouts crystal clear from the subconscious
of the passer-by.
Her offspring is chiselled to prominence in the sphere of acu-
men,
And food set on the fruits of her burns.
A warmth thus sparks her face as a smile illumines her heart,
Matching her strong in the scuffle, friends to life.

She isn't of dough, Chiefs or gods,
But Limousines cue at her fireplace to savour her work.
At the roadside she sees morning, heat and cold,
But isn't whore; her story, in the streets, isn't told.

In her is culture,
In her is strive,
In her is value and woman,
Nothing less than man and life.
She is mother, lover and giver,
A shrine, lost in the snub of society and its scribes.

FRANKLIN AGOGHO

See Me, Mother!

See the print of my step,
Softening the furrows dug by your tongue,
Whipping lines of complex on my ego,
Straightening my gaze to be fixed on the trail of woman.

See my breasts dance,
As I kick the ball, grind on all fours.
See me break the barns of the tie,
Knotted by patriarchy, eat their pie.

See me play the dress,
And wear the model to man's stage,
MAN's stage, I say, man's stage,
Where sex is sense and taste not muscles but bright brains.

See me mother, see me,
With your glasses of merit and not femme,
Cos' my body cries in a wilderness of fulfilment,
Heralding talent in the crevices of my sense.

Franklin Agogho

But let it go!

Hold slowly to old things and let in new
Petals of hope to bud on youthful stems,
For every dead stem once was a young shoot.

But until the hand moves up to the mouth,
Only words would (re-)fix the laxity of young colonised minds
But listen comrade, listen to the bard of the grassland;

Wisdom grows on grey hair_
But all that is grey here may be growing on
A maggot infested mount!

Listen comrade to the words of old age,
But lie not in squalor like the patient dog that
Hunger slew.

Patient dogs feed on carcasses,
And dream of sinking incisors down the marrows
Of a promised bone but hope often rides on tortoise' shell,

And hunger flies on eagle wings!
Wrap up the mat of sluggishness and pull back thy
Ostrich's head from old mirages, lads and lasses!

M.D. MBUTOH

Alike

If same voice calls for peace and war,
May be another should call for restrain,
Don't you think?

Should we fold hands over tired chests
And watch the cradle of mankind labour to
Death like the labourer who's got no pay?

'My woman is a tiger', Butake wrote,
But if his woman was a tiger, her man
Was surely a sucker!

Women are the descendants of Ham, it seems!
Cursed by their men's nakedness under the
Yoke of masculine sheepishness.

Let women be, let girls breathe, and boys too
Because many hands do light work— after all,
Is corn and beans not the ingredients of delectable corn-chaff?

M.D. MBUTOH

IV
OPTIMISM, MAN IN NATURE, YOUTH & THE FUTURE

devil

They call me a devil—

When life signed a pact with lack,
Damning my soul with no remorse,
Even afore my birth, true.

Take a look at my purse,
Ridden with trenches like it suffered lightning's curse.
Take a look at my home,
So cold and old, one could call it 'the devil's stroll.'
Take a look at my name,
Irrelevance spoilt it with shame.
Take a look at me,
It's true, there is nothing there to see.

They call me a devil.
Just because I took a seed from a tree?
In an era where Lords unearth yards of trees?

How am I devil?
When I strive in a lawless jungle?
It's at the foot of the chain that I struggle.

I am not of the Lions
Nor the Kite or the Tiger.
I just want to eat like those of Zion,
Though I trod with the vultures.

The Kings of the race inspire direction in my pace,
Creating context in which to show face.
And so, alien to royal blood and power,
I have no choice but to take my share, my swagger.

They call me 'the devil.'

FRANKLIN AGOGHO

For Daddy

Dirty ears hear dirty fears to stain dirty, dears.

In a wilderness of none but one,
Relegated to slaps from infant tongues,
I saw him used as a broom
To sweep off shit left unknown in the room.

From Akye to Akwokwi,
And Andek best knows his hand that gives,
His hand that gives still knows not the past tense,
His hand that gives still knocks on doors to share sense.

But there he is,
Locked up in captivity like a grave thief,
Drowned in the pit of disease not of his will.
Weh! How come he missed the treat of a king?

Unity, integrity and development spoke his words,
Though empty brains curse his lot at the crossroads.
Wellbeing, love and content dressed his self,
But deceit clothed in shame parade his name at auction stalls.

How don't we flash to the past?
When from glory we fell to dust,
When from laughter we melted into bitterness,
When from joy we clung fast to hope and steadfastness?

But in the heat of hungry stomachs and abused pockets,
Violent landlords and neighbourhood gossips in closets,
His head stayed high like UkobOgeng in motherland,
His feet stood firm in faith for Promised Land.
Many may curse, say he spent their share.
Many will rock, roll and extol that his end was sure and near.

But truth is at the mouth of the well,
Waiting to spill over and wash minds fresh.

Freedom lurks at the skirts of Justice,
Though the man wasn't a saint.
But it's true, saints live life exceptional, full of suffered caprice,
To teach masses drowned in hate and malice.

The world still loves you
We still love you
God still loves you

Franklin Agogho

I Believe

I have a distorted face,
A brave heart,
Strong faith,
And a soft mind.

Perception cried, for fate cursed me to relapse
Into foolishness, foolish belief,
And Naïve,
Naïve as kindergarten bliss,
Because I loved faith and shunned hate.

True, I don't condone vague promises,
Settled empty in the words of tired political visionaries.
I don't believe a pig pretty with lipstick,
Ugliness is ugliness even though it hides in retreat.

But I love faith and heart,
Not my fault, I was bathed and raised in sweet sounding harps,
Playing songs of love and God,
Dancing in jest that Heaven gives the best, not the worst.

So perception is perception,
Future is future,
For you choose cowards and cowardice will rule you,
And you choose love and you'll be the best fool,
Cos we all are fools.

I have a distorted face,
A brave heart,
Strong faith,
And a soft mind.

It's good enough to make me fly.

FRANKLIN AGOGHO

I Will Not Weep

I will not weep,
Because cheat stole my win.
I will not weep,
To fair maidens masked ugly with powdered skin.
I will not weep,
To them fooled of owning other's strings.
I will not weep,
To culture minding my business, bending my time to retreat.
I will not weep,
To fanfare fanning my failure, stale feelings.
I will not weep,
Corruption corrupted my chance, cast me into a desolate pit.
I will not weep,
For days generous in death, making idleness their king.
I will not weep,
Yes, all deserve the whip, not the weep.
I will not weep,
For God, only, deserves the weep.

FRANKLIN AGOGHO

Liquor

He is dazed,
Sinking down bubbles inundated in spirits.
She is crazed,
Drowning in booze seldom snoozed.
I pay a wage,
Yes, labour shunned the cage.
They seek face,
Ways suddenly seem strange.
Some swear we high on hate,
Talking in motionless face.
Spirits hum in my brain,
Invoking a storm brewed silent but strain.

You have it in your palm,
Settled at the bottom of the bottled spirit,
To drink and to win,
For life is here for the living.

But its living is livid,
Full of drawn faces, distorted
Places and echoed voices,
Drawing me from trance to nonentity.

Did you say that was living?
Franklin Agogho
The Traveller

Flush rice fields,
Romantic hilltops,
Clouds hovering in beautiful display,
And winding roads triumphing the grass fields.
The 80s blaring out of the bus' radio,
The happy madman on the roadside looking like he's practicing

voodoo,
Children playing on highways, ignoring your 'shoo,'
And mothers from farms, cherishing their hoes.

Sweet air sweeps in from the green of vegetation,
Sun rays flirt with cloud shadows,
Mud huts compete with modernism in corn plantations,
And bananas challenge palms in equal blows.

Food shows off its prowess too,
Potatoes with gari and yams on coco yams display their beauty
like pretty models.
Roosters jest to goats whilst pigs bow to the wimps of food in
abundance,
And various birds tweet hello as we speed by too.

The view from the window is a real fine stew,
Accentuated by the beauty, who in the tight bus, is rubbing by
you,
The recipe is a perfect natural dough,
The North West, a beauty, deep in Africa's bone.

FRANKLIN AGOGHO

Checking

For the first time
In her life time
She had to think,
Facing her fears without a blink.
What has she achieved?
Life!
And from her, who achieved?
Strife!

Then she realized,
And wanted to materialize
The dream of an achiever.
Then she inquired,
What was required.
And she's told
The greatest story
Of the old.

That;
Life is all about support,
Because man isn't an island
And to anchor you need a port –
So she had to take a stand; and show
Love.
That's all the bible
And Africa preached;
Love, and a come together for us and for them.

JUDE A. FONCHENALLA

Interior Corridors

In case you find the old me,
Tell me I suffer because I sluggish around then
And cannot provide for me now.
And that between me and me
My problem still remains lethargy,
Even though I walk around with amplified arms.
Arms that frail without prior attains.
I hear I am squashing at the corner of a lunch shed,
Starving when I can preserve and make that me
A hallucination.
But no way! I am there,
Or do I say I am here?
Unconscious that the difference between me and me
Is time.

Times I am neglecting to use timely
Times and times again. Even as you tell me that
I am suffering because I am misusing my time,
I laugh because I know there is still time
Even as time is closing up—
I still see me and me as worlds apart;
Never to be close, not even with time.
When you see the earlier me, tell me;
This is not the way and let me respond to you again,
'Your time has passed.'
As I actually live my past time.
Just still do it.
And let it cause me now to wail hard
For not heeding to you and 'me' then.
The time in between me and me has shrunk
And now we have me – wanting more time
When I wasted so much time.
Ask me when you see me that what's time worth

When we lack the right vehicle to move through it?
Ask!
I am laughing at you. I am feeling the pains.
The medic says I am not gaining healthcare
Because I am not refusing to pay for it
And I don't know if I have the money or not.
But I know I didn't keep it in the bank or anywhere.
I continually know I will get more with time
Before I get old.
I am actually here with the time, what do I tell me?
Within this relaying of eras,
I stand right here, on both sides of me,
Sending telex from me to me and from me to me
To circumvent me from a wrong me and for a right me
So that I am in for a better me.
If you meet me either ways tell me;
Tell me why I, now, suffer
And the role I played in getting myself here.

JUDE A. FONCHENALLA

The Lines in-between

At first, I didn't understand why
Andrew Crisci questioned if
'These are the bright young men of
Our future'
After he saw kids smoke weed.
Like him, I distrust the
Decision of handing over to them
The key of continuity.

They have refused
To raise to the bar of responsibility;
Seeking succour in bars
Like liquor consoles.
I wish someone told them
About Hardy's Henchard
And let them listen to life and Death
Of a man with character.

No one will tell you they pay tips in
Exchange for a right to chat on phone
While driving with spirits-filled brains
That confuses the red traffic light
For a faint green.
That is how innocent souls are lost
As another tip cleans the felon's sheet

You lure designers to do another finishing
On finished clothes with destructions; and
You proudly fashion it destroys.
How different will our State survive
In your care with a state of mind
Enthused by lunacy?
What a legacy! To be left to the fore-kids

We are yet to dine with our elders;
Which was the initiation to make us leaders
Not because we didn't wash our hands clean.
We actually did, but with dirty waters
And on the little sweet given us, we sweated
On it and made lines in between,
Lines that niche all that translates failure.

JUDE A. FONCHENALLA

Libel of Regrets

It's an everybody's norm. We look back
And regret at the things
We did wrong, didn't do at all – ignoring.
Wishing for another chance to right
These wrongs.
But all ends in wishes and in our heads
And our hearts that ache. It is spilled.
Trying to fix it means waiting for when
Yesterday becomes tomorrow and brings
Back the same opportunity.

Even when nature flatters and ushers with
A lookalike; it's still different and the
Same opportunity will only be a second
Time, for the first is passed and gone.

You'll be in the same spot tomorrow
If you don't stop thinking about yesterday's
Hollowness today.
Errors of the past are regrettable but not as
Regrettable as living in the past.
What memories will cloud your old age if your
Youthfulness is dead and buried in your
Childhood regrets? Regrets beget regrets.
And you will regret more if the only legacy
You ever left behind was 'Regrets'.
It is time to turn to the other page and write on
To help you ride on.

Jude A. Fonchenalla

Self-Tangle

We've been spoken to
'That if wishes were horses then,
Even beggars will ride.
True,
We've been designed beggars
But these wishes
Are negated conditionals with an 'if'.
So, do not dream these wishes:
Rather; b-live and live them
Not with posts or boasts.
But, by what you achieve virtuously.
Casuists are alert
With their neck curved earthward
Let yours neither be a bow or blow.
Be sure to see what glued
Your face onto the ground –
And not to consciously force
Your good-foot unto an idle stone.
It might just create
The lone relationship of pain
And not bring you the desired luck
'It brought others.'
The Oligarchy vacuously shortened progress' rims
But you cost yourself more for not
Knowing what you cost yourself.
You need to be sure of what
You wish for self before defining
How their commands emit you.
And on spot – in; says acceptance,
Not by terms, though, but exploits.
You've been the wanting youth;
Now, why not try the cons?

JUDE A. FONCHENALLA

The Slain Slay Queens

She read,
Poetry is Sexy and other poems
And urged me to write one
For our ladies.
I told her I couldn't;
Not when the house was still on fire.
'Not even for our African Queen?'
She asked!
Of course, I know the word does exist
And
An African Queen once existed,
But not anymore.
She was irate
And I was irater for she orated
Black pirates and rated them
Ours of the most — African Queens.
"What when wrong?"
She didn't sob.
"You,
Just like them make no part of us
Or them."
I said!
She believed so much in history
And pointed to ancestry.
On her and in her,
I looked for actualities
To substantiate, rather all I got
Were casualties
Of another that negated her.
She said,
"The world sees her as hot."
I saw the fire in her too,
Destroying
And making stains on her.

Stains they cheaply subscribed to.
Which brought the distance.
She looked at me
And I looked at her too.
She saw, in me,
Something she recognized
But in her I saw something
That antagonized
And we felt apart
That is why
My poetry couldn't transcript her
And although
She's still her mother's daughter,
Nothing was left to prove that.
All gone for in exchange of a blur path.

JUDE A. FONCHENALLA

Is it all lost?

Ask not what caused the tooth ache
But ask of what spanner can pull it off.
Because the worst choices were the best from conception,
So all is not rotten!

Ask not the teeth that chopped ulcers into
Our young brains; conversely, show us the secret to
Everlasting therapy,
So all shan't be lost!

Rely not on rotten bamboos and pecks,
For their withering carcasses are too burdensome
Already - seek ye not the living shoot in
the intestines of gravestones.

I have seen things old people did- shame? Paa!
I have heard the noise they made too - shame? Chaa!
Longevity of old carcasses above gravestones
Only starve the maggots.

M.D. MBUTOH

Holy Parifoot!

7:30am and smallish Asians pull off the
Cover over the bee hive; buckets of wind
Belch brown sweaty and shit smeared
Black and white.

Bundled fists, constantly wrinkled faces
Purring and cursing over missed shoots or
Foul play of hard-working players.
Occasional gests over sips, and time steals itself through.

12:00 noon,
The wind is in its fecundity
Loud voices of anger and anxiety—
Then, Goal!

You would think Jesus has entered
Jerusalem on a purring donkey's back—
But money has found its way into
Asian bag, and foul mouths sing away destinies!

9:45 pm,
And expectant eyes are tilted towards the
East from whence cometh the greedy stem
Of Holy Pari-foot! Well done, tomorrow is another day.

M.D. MBUTOH

No Longer at Ease

Pull it ov'r let's have a friendly jab!
Would you sell your most cherished bird to the silence
Of the civil strife in your stomach if you knew its entrails gestate
With gold of the finest glint?

Would you abort the seed of your groin to escape
The pangs and grunts of poverty if you knew your foetus
Would be the wealthy messiah to the abjectness that
Gnaws your ribs and sucks every pore in your muscles?

Be ye no longer at ease, comrades!
Harken not to the old lie that cements thy athletic feet in the
Dust of your ailing forebears – your fingers, your head, your
eyes,
Your body, your every being– they are precious gifts from the
Gods.

M.D. MBUTOH

Are you Ready?

You whose prayers shoot needles
Into the hooves of the elephant,
Are you ready?

You who foam with liquor
When the cock is yet to wake up,
Are you ready to crow along?

You, whose penis hangs over the door
Frame like an old blind, touching every
Female visitor, are you done with your coitus?

You, the sheet, who rant over the hotel servant's slowness
To turn over the old sheet,
Wash your nicotine stench with wisdom, and skills.

Are you ready, you who have a ready name for
Every incompetency— do you have the skills of
Joseph gathered with perspiration and years?

M.D. Mbutoh

A Taxi Ride

My legs bore my tired trunk to the beehive
Of the Union Palace whence it took me ages to board
A limping taxi.

And the giant iron ran from right to left
Of the tar-scarce capital road

"Trois cent Chapelle Obili!"

It spurned its bottom like a dangerous damsel in the
Crest of the night at Mini Ferme desperate for some franc,
and halted with a rustic screech.

And the giant iron ran from right to left
Of the tar-scarce capital road

I scampered in like a rat mole disappears into
The intestines of the earth when the sun's lids creak.
A stench of dirt and vomit slapped me squarely.

And the giant iron ran from right to left
Of the tar-scarce capital road

The driver, a scarce bearded fellow in early thirties
Sweat-smeared collar laid carelessly behind a
Choppy African neck.

And the giant iron ran from right to left
Of the tar-scarce capital road

One fleshy hand searched frantically amid papers,
Another gripped the steering wheel and his brown
Teeth bit an old cell phone.

And the giant iron ran from right to left
Of the tar-scarce capital road, then bwamm!

"Oh gush! Terrible road! Biya is to blame!" curses poured
Easily out of his mouth as tyres screeched and scampered
Out of a giant pothole.

And the giant iron ran from right to left
Of the tar-scarce capital road

"Did Biya ask you to do a thousand things
While driving?"
It was my neighbour sailing on a silent pool of anger.

And the giant iron ran from right to left
Of the tar-scarce capital road.

Then at Province, the machine grunted to a halt
Before a dirty plank cupboard and he pulled his
Weight out, counted currencies and exchanged with Parifoot
ticket!

Tchap! Tachaptchap!
Garadik! Garadik! Garadik!
Ignition kicked to live, two or three throttles, then Chapelle
Obili here we are!

And the giant iron ran from right to left
Of the tar-scarce capital road

M.D. MBUTOH

A Generation without Vision

When in a society greetings
Are measured on a ceremonial seat
And numbers of fake red feathers you
Count on corrupt heads, it is a society whose
Vision grew wings and migrated.

When youth go sober before the cock crows,
And students eat old beards for lunch and dance
On vigorous pestles all nights, it is a society
Where norms are aliens and the Ngumba has
Become a friend of laziness in broad day robbery.

A society without vision grows its vegetable on
Yesterday's urine spattering in fiery droplets
Like excited houseflies enjoy beautiful games on
Fresh dungs. It is a society that has lost its vision
Like the careless virgin's virginity.

It is a generation with plenty of vision, indeed—
In an old wagon that rolls its tyres on decrees and communiqués,
Vision stolen in dreams and nightmares jumping from
Sexagenarians to octogenarians and to nonagenarians; a furious
Pollutant settling from hymen to hymen.

Sell-outs scampering aboard grunting plastic
Shells in the Mediterranean, competing with sharks
While vision is forever buried in the earth's womb and hidden
dungeons
With the memories of the dead, the martyrs of sane discord—
Repressive hands, old pitiless claws clipping young ambition's
wings.

M.D. Mbutoh

V
MIGRATION, PROTEST
&
CALL TO DUTY

Exodus

The Lord says, 'Let My people go.'
Let the people go.
Let the fatherless baby of the raped mother whose parents lost
their heads go,
Let them go.

It isn't their fault,
That they seek a new promised land, a Vault,
Where they will lay heads in heaven's peace, no fault.

It is easy to claim the stand
That the pyramid, tall, wouldn't rise without sparing grains of
sand.
But what happens when strange winds blow off these grains,
grand?
Will the pyramid still rise to command?

Too easy it is to engrave,
That we aren't in error, didn't pre-dig their graves,
Didn't make them slaves,
Just were better than them at fair trade,
And so have no game shading their heads.

Fair trade, truly fare?
When souls roam the wilderness in the shadow of crazy fauna?
Hell No!
Let them go,
Let them live,
Let them stay.
The earth was where they were born.

Can't you hear the lamentations of the dead boy at the sea shore?
It rings in my ears.

I thought we were free?

FRANKLIN AGOGHO

My Writer

Wielding the carrot and the stick,
Bending blind bones to moral breathing,
Defines her skill, his calling,
Though creative souls sleep deep in the graves of their workings.

Knives and yam sit warm in the bag,
To heal the soul, feed the lack,
But pots cursed the smith,
Scaring naked fires to shun the seed, hiding their heat.

Soldier at war with pen and ink,
Shooting stained paper at the enemy,
Corrupt contemporaries, slaves to pop culture,
Leaving word casualties in the throats of illiterate vultures.

Yes, my writer.

FRANKLIN AGOGHO

Retribution

While wavy waters wash waste wide with wrath,
Do not expect tear-filled streets
To Shine with pride,
When like raided tombs,
Their core has been wasted,
Shaking essence madly into despair.

Retribution is at the doorstep.

FRANKLIN AGOGHO

Zion: Home

Hollow skulls churn on the floors of the Mediterranean
As brothers sleeping in sub zeroed streets,
Beholding sisters weeping on bruised groins
And others caged in Arab holes, seek home at the first exit.

Bones sing the sad song in the sands of the Sahara
For brothers roaming the fruitful streets of motherland,
Loading lost bags on the sweat of family's weak reserve
For a death walk to ruins in the heart of sandy wilderness.

Ancestors weep to eulogy-borne planes,
Flying in sons lost to lunacy,
Who escaped their fatherland of streets full of plenty,
Ravished by the few, by the savvy.

A gong heralds a call to Zion, Home,
Trembling with eruptions of milk and honey,
Caged in cracked rocks at the bottom of alacrity,
For souls of the witty, souls of the bold.

Home is Zion and Zion is Home,
Chew down adversity and build the throne.

Franklin Agogho

Burial of the Patient Dog

For shame's sake,
Let old bones rest and young bones be buried—for once!
Have you heard, brother?
The patient dog wandered beyond the bad reaper's boundary!

For shame's posterior's sake,
Let old bones rest and young bones be buried!
Have you heard, sister?
Adult children ate the patient dog's bones!

For sanity's plea,
Put old libraries back into the annals of museums
And new books shall drink the dust of their
Forebears like hyenas trace the trails of old games.

Let's pray, brothers—
You hear this coarse shaky voice too, sister?
Thrust poverty-infested hands towards God's house
And let us pray for the soul of old pants lost in their

Bafia rigmarole-like nyanguup, fallen into a bowl of sand!
When a drum has an ulcer, you take it back to the owner,
When an egg is fallen, you take it back to the nest;

So take this soul into the cold womb of the earth!
But not just yet dear Jehovah of the Jews.
Take not this soul into the beauty of your kingdom, dear
Nkalang of the Peuchop people!

Let us pray the last prayer of the last requiem of Bate Besong,
For there shall be overflow of palm wine into the heads of
Those who wait for the shoes of the young people!

A tree has never grown with its head into the sweet
Warmth of mother earth's hymen,
For an iroko tree will not grow beyond the sheens of clouds
Beneath God's soles,

Tune us dear brother—tune and prune these young shoot to
beauty,
Tune us dear sister—work these maiden wires to good melodies,
And we shall resurrect the soul of the patient dog from
Slumber, yet, not the way octogenarians regurgitate bad blood.

But in the honest ways of hard work:
No more sycophants of dead bones— for we intend to make
Libraries and unbeatable museums out of these dry bones,
Resurrect the mummies old Alexandria, read of the Hieroglyph-
ics

From the laps of grand temple of Njoya's Scripts
Like Ndeh Ntumazah dislocated the jaws of colonialism!
We have come to bury not the lazy soul of the patient dog,
But to resurrect the lava in its heart.

M.D. Mbutoh

Let's Be Honest for Once!

In this village, the gums of sages say that
A woman desperate for a child does not go to bed
Dressed like she is on a war front,

So let's be honest, at least for once!
Our youth have become a shadow of young stem,
They have become hollow phloem through which old maggots
feed.

Let's be honest, at least for once!
At 7a.m. alcohol makes its steam in the eyes of young ambition
And drains every iota of hope like wick sucks of kerosene.

At 7a.m a flush of "33" bulldozes its way down the throats
Of virgin forests, uprooting undergrowth ere their heads
Are raised beyond the foliage of gaunt barks.

Let us look into the mirror in a pinch of sincerity, comrades!
We have sat on the shit that came out of our own anuses
And have carried flies with us for decades like shadows follow
our earths.

Let's face fact like heroes face their fears.
When at 7:30 a.m. we scramble and make our seats in Parifoot
Halls and bask in the successes of foreigners, when do we plant?

For once, let's chew our own tails and succumb to our shame!
When our mirages fly in the skies of social media,
Polluting genuine smiles with poisonous dust of fake news—
when, do, we, work?

For once, face the rhythm of our own hollow beats
Like the kangaroos dance to the rigmarole of their steps;
Easy lies the head that shall be crushed!

M.D. MBUTOH

Slippery Hope

When you watch hope slip through
The gaps between your blister-infested fingers,
And your ears listen to the grunts of poverty excavating
A lion den in your stomach, the awe of vagabond
Won't leave you in peace

When your silhouette grows gaunter
At the peak of the mammoth hill resting
At the back of your hut, and your eyes travel lazily
Across the seven hills of your shack to the villas of your
Former mates, the riot in your chest curses your manliness.

When you look at the twine round your lice-infested
Waist and see the line of rashes building up new
Frog backs round your genitals, the pangs of shame
Push your hands to hold destiny by its horns—
And when the tax collector feeds by your sweat,
Hope slips over your young old shoulder with a blink.

M.D. Mbutoh

When you Leave Home

When you leave home and familiarity hides its face in a
Dark corner as mere litter of beautiful dirt on your mind,
The sand of time is blown by the winds of worries, it leaves you
At the crossroad when the pain of age bites your muscles;

Your issues breathe foreign air
Like new shoots uprooted from the warmth of Africa,
They're new nuts planted in the womb of cold Americas et al.

When you leave home, the sand of time can slip through
The gaps of your fingers while you watch over it, locked in the
Shackles of worries and the inconsistencies of existence.

The sand of time simmers gradually into maturity
Like the hearth boils nuts to turgidity with each glow;
A loud sound of furious bubbles and rigorous pursuance,
Then no more!

When you leave home
The way the baby leaves the womb,
The confused blows of life whirl round you,
So intense you would wish to dive back into the womb.

M.D. MBUTOH

Sea Fairing

Night meetings in tall towers,
Careless words falling lazily into media's ears,
Suited bald skulls costumed in affability and potent
Handshakes poised to put meat into the sharks'
Mouths and rid European streets of undesirables,

Their Excellency recline their unconcerned thrones
Over frothing skulls and teary eyeballs of bartered souls,
And told the world how poor they have become!

At the head of a poor community
Standing over billion gallons of rich oil
In the suburbs of a deserted land in the north,
Terrorists feast the maturity of fresh ransom!

They drum their chests and dance the baboon dance
Over memories of shackled ṣub-Saharan black fists,
... another successful operation in the marketplace!
Boom!

Buses packed full with terror-stricken
Faces grunting and drifting down south
Forests, and green helmets soak the
Silent land like desert water.

Pieces of sweaty loins
Litter the Saharan desert, playing the scarecrows,
Mummifying every daring soul—
But even fear too is dead!

In the abyss of a gaping Mediterranean fangs,
Large man-eating beasts file their canines and
Practice the noosing of sea-fairing preys perched
Over rubber shells with grunting engines.

M.D. Mbutoh

VI
NEOCOLONIALISM, MENTAL ENSLAVEMENT, INTELLECTUAL DEBASEMENT, & NATIONHOOD

Angels

Gauging from every vantage point,
They hover in proud fare,
Dusting even the speckle off their collars,
Bouncing like the earth was their birth mate.

They kill with their tongues,
Sparing none from the whip of their words,
Driving many to enmity faster than they thought
And leaving more living corpses than dead humans to walk.

'Did virtue truly die?' we hear their earnest cry.
'Why all the caging in the backrooms of financial banks?'
'How come the farmer doesn't feed on his harvest?'
'Oh God, humanity has tossed essence into the middle of the
desert.'

Many smile at their bright smiles,
Their clean kisses and their blatant slaps.
They are redemption in the eyes of the world,
True angels, come to represent the Lord.

But hierarchy stepped in one day,
Crowding the populace so much, even Reason had no say.
Eyes get blinded just at the sight of collar roses,
angels suddenly shy like lions laying cowardly quiet in the poul-
try farm.

The fear to tell the truth has crowded their very core
For the truth has a price tag,
A sensitive price with bigoted roots
Which can bring poverty so ferociously like an angry storm.

Corruption now lurks the streets in embezzling romance.
Nepotism, in the best suits, parade high and low corridors.
The people are crying, 'Oh angels, why?'
And in reply, 'we will do right but we can't change their style.

FRANKLIN AGOGHO

Bait

They throw us bait,
Like we were fish,
Waiting to be wasted whilst we wish our wishes.
They throw us bait,
In eleven dashing behind inflated leather,
Hoping we were seduced by breasts in t-shirts,
And drank our history, our future, in momentary thrills and
beer steads.

They throw at us,
Like lusty elders, gods,
Pouring palm wine at the town crier,
Shivering at the melodious gong,
Cos' its sweet tune will corrupt innocent ears, truth songs.

They threw,
Hoping we wouldn't apprehend the hue,
Of darkness kept for smaller twin,
And hoped,
That Esau will laugh rash,
So Jacob wouldn't seed a nation of kings.

And it is true,
Their baits were lodged in extra-large throats,
Fed fat on false hope,
Excited at the rope, not even the hook.
Yes, they throw us bait,
But we wouldn't ravel in skinny worms,
But swim to ours, fish, even through the storm.

FRANKLIN AGOGHO

Jungle Justice

There they are, seated on their thrones,
Clapping to the show like it was a joker's jest.
Kill him, Kill him, they cry,
As they hunger for blood painting death on living flesh.

I saw the saw cut the nail on the stone platform,
To host autopsy on his life, no anaesthesia,
No pity on the judges smiling with grudging faces,
Bent on playing God, building hell on rubber's reject.

O Christ, what was his crime?
To fill the gap borne by their theft?
Their incompetence?

They say he stole sugar
Meant to sweeten the mouths of the blasphemers
Who preach blossom to dirty ears
In a world plunged in hell.

There they are, fat as inflated balloons,
Seating on dark thrones which hide away
Dreams grown old on despair,
Which, like slaves, fertilize their ego; false strength.

The populace, they used the hammer,
Soothed his wounds with salt,
Like the saviour, adorned his skin in whips,
Crucifying his frame in a pit of flames.

So they joyed the end of his struggle,
Illegitimate as it was.
But was the thief truly crucified
In a crowd soaked in masked lies?

The roots grow tentacles, so the tree stands firm.

FRANKLIN AGOGHO

Midnight and Five

It was at three,
Midnight and three,
When you told me—
Told me to share mine which was mine.
It was midnight and three,
And I had to choose from oui and thine.

Now we prude, exclude and mute,
Rant at shared bedding meant for two,
And shout in the deep night safe for you.
You cup my screams in your drenched hands,
Forced to belly a contract of love turned wrong.

God!
You raked my groins,
Dug my insides like worms going through rot boils,
Drained the milk from my milkless breasts full of milk,
Painted red your lust for power over the bed,
Because I screamed stop and you heard yes.

But it is five, not midnight, but five.
The kids stare at the day wake, it's five,
And your rapture will stop, cos' neighbours stare with benign
eyes.
It is five, and my screams bark into the dreams of the passers-by,
Listing your thrusts on the list of threat to human life.
STOP!

FRANKLIN AGOGHO

Suits

Sometimes laziness wears blue,
Blazing its beauty on a red tie.

Franklin Agogho

Trend

I am terrified
By the way they treat trend.
Feels like whatever crosses the heart is good to send
To the world as an open letter of freedom,
That even terror can call a peaceful kingdom.

FRANKLIN AGOGHO

Wind the glass

The streets are filled
With boys in shackles,
Girls in belly balloons,
Children waving insult-speaking robots,
All on the leash of the old man's strength lagoon.

Wind the glass and see,
Pale souls with filled trays
Of hope screaming despair,
Of chance dreaming de bon air,
And bodies eager to push out babies with grown heirs.

Wind the glass and feel
The cold of words of old,
The glee and spree of hope,
Built on the weariness of hearing
'We can't do all things with a strength so glaring.'

Wind the glass and touch
Chains on bodies like colts,
Trotted by mind-stagnating cults
Whose preys cry in a crowded wilderness,
For wills to wipe their cold sweatiness.

Wind out of fortune and listen
To your name, searching for purpose and action,
Because the streets are filled with boys in shackles,
Girls in belly balloons,
And children waving at you to be more than a chauffeured cartoon.

FRANKLIN AGOGHO

Amongst Us

When the South refused to join the North,
It positioned the fifty-three like hard pillars
Of salt, and the results were upheavals
As the three threatened and finally structure self to four;
And now five, six and other numbers
Getting unnumbered inspirations.

We refused to pride ourselves
As a self,
The counsel to stand as one strong man
Against a few weak Men
Who have gained force in our divides and minds
Because we sold out as over fifty individuals.

We have sold-out with no string attached.
Ignore our cousin's cattle ranchos
To go starve on chemical milk, far from home.
And in return gain 'confirmation into civilization'
While our cousin abandon the course
And the healthy cows give way for the bones.

We have lost us, in the culture,
While bargaining to be them in their subcultures
Of fashion, disrespect and misdemeanours.
Their lives shaping our lives
And their colour and wigs becoming our preferences,
Yet we sit, amongst us, and blame only leaders.

Their strength is permanent
In our ideas to be in their like image
While they depart from God's golden image
Making us shadows of selves chasing ghosts.
Let's repair it amongst us
And continue back to the road of yesteryears.

Jude A. Fonchenalla

After all the Noise

They will tell you how precarious the path is:
"Lions' tails are shelters"
Impatient voices would say.
But harken not to the voice of deceit and discouragement.

Storms and plagues don't last forever!
The beauty of storms lies in their ravages,
But the elegance of success, too, flirts on thorny
Paths traced by the fury of monumental failures.

Each time at the top of a ladder, the retrospection of a
Glance amounts the joys of a successful heart
By the scent of its vapour, then, the quality of faeces is known.

After all the noise comrade, remember the waves have never
Cut a swimmer; navigate through and dust yourself like the
Ducks shake off blobs of water into the palms of a faithful sun.
Noises never move the lions' tails from the path of its hunt.

M.D. Mbutoh

Age of Mirage

Gone is the age when truth
Looked you in the face with defiant
Scrawl of wisdom,

Gone are those days when parents tied noose
Of truth and wore bangles of sincerity—
Lost days evaporated like morning dews!

Because we have sailed on dyslexia's wings
And drunk of octogenarian gallons of wine, that now
Teams upstairs like a foaming glass of Bordeaux.

The age of mirage deceives the eyes,
Nothing seems the ordinary, and hearts jump
In the middle of city heat like maggots in cesspit.

M.D. MBUTOH

Coats of Sugar

Crumps of sugar shredded in
The marketplace and sows sniff
The ensnared broth whence jingles of
Death lure like a ring on a sow's snot.

Coats of sugar wrapped in hypocritical
Cocoyam leaves have started to emit signals
Of venoms and pus.

A light coat of perfume lingers over
Schools of maggots and intestinal faeces,
Whiteth sepulchre!

Smokescreen rising up on feast days like monstrous
Silhouettes of sails on the calm nerves of the sea,
They build gigantic chasms of ice in the air.

M.D. Mвuтoн

Dying...

My village is on a keg of powder
That's gone badly,

There have been much fury
And rubbing... and the thunder
Has lost its patience!

My village is on a keg of
Smoky powder

There have been much cacophony
And the scuffle... spilled the powder
On the splint!

My village is dying, dying like
A cancer patient left to itself,

Birds pass overhead and stare
In horror as lances fall carelessly on
Toes and fingers of Rwanda 94!

My village is dying,
It is a grey turf drifting into withering coma!
A coma of intellectual pneumonia.

M.D. MBUTOH

Empty Cans and Fart Collectors

Long caskets snake through
Ministerial streets droning like
Giant dragons in monstrous ecstasy.

Multi-pieces of enormous blankets
Clad round his excellency's mammoth
Bowels like Japanese sumo wrestlers'

Empty cans follow his excellency into toilets
And collect his farts with affable smiles:
"Merci mon papa le ministre !"

Young people have become tools to chew
Political opponents that rejuvenate old age
In youthful laps.

M.D. MBUTOH

Frugality

Two poor knees on the stomach of a silent soil is better
To a fon over a teary belly licking the dust like a serpent.
The earth breathes life into every marrow and nurses
Every hurting veins with the tenderness of a grandmother's
breasts.

So walk tall in the glow of majesty and defiance,
Though thy stomach may be a lion's den now, the beasts
Shall sing your praise in the tongues of Daniel's lions
In the dungeons of a frustrated king of ignorance and jealousy.

Take up the mantle and map the breathing ground with
A defiant stroke of a master
Inscribe your initials on the wall like fingers wade
Off old containers.

Frugality is the nutrient of young buds in the scorch of
Harmattan, interspersing into the locks of drought and
Occasional drizzles of kind evening tears that
Chop the particles of dust with swords of perseverance!

M.D. Mbutoh

Mediocrity

Mediocrity is a mount on which
Poverty makes its nest slowly and surely—

Mediocrity paves the streets with pebbles of buffoonery,
Fried beignets wreathed in plastic by graduates...

Graduates—bags full of certificates and foamed heads full of
theories
And treated leprous truth, systematically buttressed in young
skulls.

Mediocrity hides itself in the bars and snacks
And beckons at half-coated youthfulness.

Mediocrity is a metal that magnets promiscuity—
Years of varsity sacrifices seep gracefully down "33" bottles.

Mediocrity falls off archaic mouths under rusty varsity
Zinc and sandwiched by stone walls—Africa's intellectual Bastille!

Large corrupt mouths smog at youthful faces
And fill empty cans with civilised frustrations.

M.D. MBUTOH

Powder and Hatred

Hatred is a keg of gun powder,
Hatred is a volcano enshrouded two inches
beneath the hairy pores of mobile pillars.

There is a village in the armpit of
The whiteman's death trap,
Yesterday it was the whiteman's dead trap,

Today we have made it ours,
Under the shadows of sceptres and
Commanding staff, we reign with iron fists

Stealing from our own bags
And nodding beneath the applause of the aliens,
Hatred is the gun powder given freely to us

To keep the panthers that eat at day
Instead of nights but we hunt even at
Night!

M.D. Mвитон

VII
WAR, TERRORISM
&
STRIFE

Desert Girl

Fatima,
Her name is Fatima.
A desert girl, tender,
Born to a family of splendour,
Basking life, simple in its purpose.

She loves the trade of day,
Strolling in father's cattle and sheep bleating in array.
She loves mother's way,
Hoeing grain and spinning milk which she brings to mature
ways.

Pestles beat grain to obedience before her eyes.
She puts her scarf in place to spy,
Her cousins pounding in elegant rhythm,
Grain to dust, in the mortar's prism.

She loves the play too,
Clapping dances in sand and swaying feet in no shoes,
Throwing stones puts a smile on her face
And catching them in company baits solace.

Quiet!
She's closed her eyes to pray.
Allah is here, no play.
It's with love that she pays homage to God,
And prays for peace, and family to be strong.

In a veil, the market is her best destination,
Marvelled by cloth of colours from all locations,
Spices accompanying women of cultures from diverse regions,
And beauty tattoos painted on hand and feet which are precious.

She runs to the town square,
To relish the city's glare.
Then suddenly,

EXPLOSION!

Flames and fumes steal the air,
Wails, panic and sirens capture the terrain,
The sun is blotted out of the sky.

Fatima,
A tender desert girl,
Is now flesh, bones and blood,
Spread out on the sands of the Sahel.

FRANKLIN AGOGHO

Ghosts

It's there, in the air.
It's there, on the dusty roads.
Listen, they're there in the potholed streets.

Can't you see?
They browse and process faceless with deep eye sockets and hollow mouths,
Scaring parading uniforms screeched with armed gas,
Who look but can't see.

Listen again.
They scream in halls full of gone souls,
Souls resting in the cosiness of their home graves,
Souls deaf to cries from corrupt lips,
Lips cracked deep with the fails of defeat.

Keep calm, Listen.
The souls parade the empty streets,
And they scream,
Victory, VICTORY!
The dead souls beaten to life now shine through God the King.

Listen,
The souls parade the empty streets,
And fear steers the hearts of cheap chiefs.

Franklin Agogho

I Saw, Now I See

I saw him tie his boots,
Crawl into the greenish plane like a shadow stabbed with a hook.
I saw him put the arm in place and prepare for shots,
Staring in half fear, wondering if it's worth the trust.
I saw him get into rank,
Obeying orders from the General who can't prance.
I saw him chant the songs,
And rush into the battlefield, to fight not man but thoughts.
I saw him laugh in wait,
Hoping the enemy feared the display and escaped.
I saw him watch the first attack,
Dragging his blood-soaked comrade to the back.

Then,
Bullets flew, bombs blasted and drones spied,
Skulls opened, limbs yanked and heads rolled,
Famine threatened, babies died with culture, lost,
And towns evaporated, with bombs strapped to the chest of children, not thoughts.
I see him gaze at death,
Noticing how worthless human life can be for some, right from birth.
I see him stare at his daughter's tender face,
Imagining her crawling away from blasts like those under his case.
I see him see politicians,
Drinking diplomatic champagne in diplomatic chant.
I see him see the poor and underprivileged,

And realising that religion was never the battle's urge.
I see a man who knows man,
And is ready to give all to make man stand.
I see a hero, a star and a monument,
I see the reason why many, still, are able to open their mouths
and laugh.

FRANKLIN AGOGHO

Madmen and Guns

A madman has the gun, brother!
Restrain from your ranting, comrade!
For a madman has got the gun now.

Watch out brother, for petals of blood
Rain over the roof and the oceans are rising
To kiss the maddening heavens.

It is a dark day, comrade!
Darker than the capitol warning of Caesar,
Have you seen the majestic lion parade the silent square?

Millions of voices cry in the womb of the graves,
And hastily woven covers threaten to break,
Hold your peace brother, for a madman got hold of the gun!

M.D. MBUTOH

Blind Justice!

Ministry of justice;
One for you one for me and the
Land is good!

Petals of blood falling in gutters
Never to evaporate again,
Down with secessionists!

They create their lies,
They invent their truths and
Believe in them all!

How can a terrorist be victim of
His own actions?
Petals of blood sprinkling on cold tarmac!

M.D. Mbutoh

Blood in their Hands!

Wrapped in iron cloth and warmed
On the flames of anger,
Then shoved into your throat,
That is their truth!

Listen comrades,
Listen to the sound of the distant
Drums calling for revellers
Of enlightenment dancing with

Masked faces down the hill.
They will be defeated, so says the
Supreme commander of the undertakers,
Hear the petals of their blood drop in silence.

Perfection is confirmed in the grave,
Hear the voice of the racing panther
Sailing down into the valley of
The goddess of the river Mongolo.

M.D. MBUTOH

Playing Chaplin

If they allowed you to play
The Chaplin for this long,
It's because time was worth wasting.

But the worms mock at the follies
Of time and mask needs with urgency.
For youthfulness is pruned to pruning.

But the play's run sour after whirling
Round Sisyphus' stone for close to two
Scores of casting words, eating words,

Regurgitating words and pushing them
Down the itching throats of sycophants:
"Youth of today, leaders of tomorrow!" Taa!

But the song may change its lyrics when
Grandparents close hazy brows and hide
In plantain stems—"beggars today, debtors
Tomorrow"

M.D. MBUTOH

Forget the old Lies!

Leave the old lies for the hearts that liveth in
The dark womb of the past and trek forward
In the strides of young kings and princes.

Let lie the old lies fanned with palm fronds of
Falsehood and political demagogy - "youth in the morning
Shall be ripe in the ev'ning!" Paa!

Don't fall for cheapness of such subtleness,
For even God's word was adulterated to give
Slavery an angelic face.

Let not the rigidity of old octogenarian falsehood
Placate the today against yest'day like an 80-year-old
Scrotum slings like sucker beneath old butts.

Forget the old lies, young lads and lasses!
Flap your wings in the sombre pupils of a young
Sun and drink in the morning clouds with the swallows.

M.D. MBUTOH

VIII
WISDOM, STEWARDSHIP, REDRESS, SPIRITUALITY, & IDENTITY

Age is Gold

In the folds of his skin I see gold,
In the wrinkles of her eyes I see most bright,
In the feebleness of his limbs I see strength,
Still bearing life, carrying it on his shoulders with brio.

At the front door, under the cypress tree, shading the blinding
sun,
He told me the story leaning on his cane, puffing smoke with
ease, his life,
That he dodged bullets in bloody escape, world war,
Danced gramophone in independence songs,
Wed the sweet mother whose eggs multiplied strong,
And witnessed power tussle power and gain forte.

On her back lay the trace of weight,
Imposed relentless by life, the sure race,
To feed the young, mould the weak,
And assure the brave that life is not to take with greed.

But I see the powdered face teen snob
As her crumpled smile cheers with counsel,
Because he is as strong as a military Lieutenant,
Warding off his ways of old,
Swearing that fresh crops don't grow best on an old farm
And forgetting that swift engines grew tough on old ones.

Age is Gold!

FRANKLIN AGOGHO

Blind

It seems you don't know
that light never squabbles with darkness
over trivialities buried in the void
of life, shaped in the form of the shapeless truth
that can't become a lie.

FRANKLIN AGOGHO

Him

Cosy on the laps of mother's warmth,
Staring blind into the Book's words,
Singing hymns in father's tune,
Was how I came to know of You.
Almighty, All Powerful, All Seeing,
Imagining you hidden behind the sanctuary's screen,
Staring at our thoughts through the heavy cross,
I thought of You discarding our loss.
Heavenly Shepherd, Our Father, Our King,
I still wondered throughout Sunday school's bliss,
Why in Shepherd's need you didn't come to steal the sheep,
Turning my thoughts into a servant allegiant to sleep.
Sleep, my escape into a world of dream,
For in destitute our lives were sealed,
Forging despair as the cutlass to clear pauperism,
In a world permanently glued to a stop mechanism.
Oh! We cried a confused cry,
I, confused, cried but didn't understand why,
For in faith I awaited the Hand of the Father
But it seemed to have travelled away even farther.
My hands, I wondered if they were too soiled with sin,
Too soiled to be seen in this dark abyss,
Till father made clear the statement,
'God's time is best in patience.'
In years I've come to marry the assertion,
God's time is best, yes, in patience.
For, over time, generous in number,
His Hand has reached me times beyond number.

FRANKLIN AGOGHO

Roots

I eat roasted plantains,
Swimming in palm oil,
Settled in a wooden bowl, no lid,
In a kitchen soothed with smoke in increase,
And grandmother uttering stories of We.

That is me,
That is who I am,
That's origin,
The mother of cultural stance.

I'm harmattan,
Dust is my daily abode.
I'm bare feet, bare- bodied and eating with hands,
Earth is where I explode.

I live because I know me,
And because I know me,
I'm free like a searching kite,
Soaring over the grassland and seeing every mice.

So don't define me,
Without me, I'm not me,
Because I cannot see what I can't see.
How do you want me to be you?
And still remain me and true?
You give me names,
Tell me to tame
The life I live, you claim is lame,
And embrace shame to gain fame.

Look at what you've done,
My brothers have all gone
Into war, suffering and exile,
Because they no longer know who they are.

The definition of me
Only rests in my roots.

How do you define definition when its definition is already defined?

FRANKLIN AGOGHO

The Joker

I jolted out of a dream
Of I, chauffeur-driven by death,
To the town of heaven's hell,
With smiling faces, parading with stained shirts,
Red.

Red kisses of sliced flesh on the leash of the scythe,
Singing praises to the mount,
Where the prophet shouts.
The prophet,
White faced, red lipped, eyes of a puppet,
The joker, smiling like a wild Muppet.

'Repent, the end is on your nose,' I saw him smile,
Looked like that guy on the card,
Opened bible in his hands,
And little chubby angels swinging like chaps,
Sullen by despair of unfulfilled tasks.

Truly, despair rode on souls,
Marching to the road leading to the lake of bread,
The lake of cakes and beer bubbles,
Shunning the lake of water,
And singing praises just to the glamor of the joker's sweat.

'Repent, Repent,' he smiled once again,
And some smiled into water,
Beaming at the others in cake,
Filling their pockets, stuck on the opulence of their round selves,
Proud at the health of their take.

Then a fire, then a gas, then explosion,
And hands, bowels and excretion.
Then faces, then bones, then blood,
Then I jolted to the TV, a preacher sang a song.

'Beware, beware, I see doom,'
'False filled pockets may wail in gloom,'
'They will laugh at the truth and extol,'
'I am sure my words laugh like a joker's jokes.'

I rubbed sleep away,
Let me eyes see the way,
Then I understood it whole,
We think God is a Joke.

I dropped to my knees.

Franklin Agogho

The Rooster

On the country sides where the country boasts bright sides,
Merging love and culture in a trunk.
There, where man, machine and farmer share strides,
A rooster jests its strength bare and strong.

In military beauty it steps in pride,
A proud patriot stepping on its forefather's path.
In the tunes of the breeze that sweeps grass green on the hill-
sides,
The rooster scratches to view grain sprinkled by nature's hand.

Clad in feathery handsomeness,
It dances in rainbow colours protruding its chest.
Singing maleness in its morning crow,
Hens rush to grow eggs cuddled in its bow.

It is polygamous!
Capping its crowned aura in the spirit of a feathered sage.
But they adhere,
Leading silvery chicks to the image of their love.

Like a war god,
It barricades its territory, feeding all equal in fill.
Like a son of its fathers,
It threatens to drench confused crowers losing their place and
speed.

The rooster,
A true son of kings.

FRANKLIN AGOGHO

Deadline

Align with a craft,
And wait if the prophecy comes true,
And takes you through
Life's draft.
Focus will guide those dreams;
Boiling like magma awaiting explosion
And will trim
Those anxieties that lead to frustration.

Deadline
Shouldn't be a dream's death line.

JUDE A. FONCHENALLA

Supports

Support,
A supposed lending of consciousness,
To pull the others to the level
Of their wishes, but,
Maybe, not consciousness
That is our own forte system
Helping us out of misery to achieve together.
Operation holding hands to surety ours.
Why support,
When freely giving opposes
Supporters and their innateness,
Including their gifts.
Should it just spring like time?
What is there to support with all the will to do so?
When all their choices available bleed values
And hypes what humanity decries.
Are we to support meritocracies?
And let substandard take a tick?
What then do we do when standard shows up?
Pity and re-enact our let-go culture?

JUDE A. FONCHENALLA

Dreams and Drums

Dreams are gari with which the sugary
Will to eat shall let those who flex thirst
Of its aroma and think of future dreams with delight.

Dreams are seeds planted with determination,
Watered consistency and positivity, and weeded with
Vigilance and care

If the squirrel can sow nuts for laziness to prey on,
Surely youthfulness can sow for old age to plough
And fret!

But fret not their withering souls over a running
Brook, in the laps of giant feet forest down the stomach
Of ancestral bosom.

Dreams are drums:
The hand that beats it down shall enjoy
The rhythm of its melody in the feet of passers-by!

Dreams are drums,
You can beat out any melody: lullaby, dirge,
Lyrics, symphony, ode, etc.

M.D. MBUTOH

Glass Houses

Beware of glass houses with opaque souls
Masked in large white pieces of clothes like
Sugared vinegar,

Beware of mirthful embraces,
Great plants to redress the leaking thatches,
And give the world a facelift—

Fall not for conjurers of mirages,
Tongues that build chasms of glasses,
Y-tongues that sting and relish youthfulness to immobility.

Beware of the soles of time!
For these things were told to us by martyrs who bled
At the pulpit whence destinies were inked on yellow leaves.

Those who dwell in glass houses have souls hollow
With the tales of nothing,
Vacuumed souls pinned on the butts of history.

Beware of legs,
Legs that walk backward— they walk
Right into the excrements of history!

M.D. MBUTOH

ABOUT THE AUTHORS

Franklin Agogho is an award-winning writer from the North West Region of Cameroon. His short story, *The Curse* won first prize in a national contest organized by Cameroon's Ministry of Arts and Culture (2016). His works have appeared in *Bakwa Magazine, Brittle Paper* and *AfricAvenir*. His debut comic book, *Totem* was published in 2019 by Zebra Comics Inc. He holds an MA

in International Relations and a BA in English Modern Letters. Franklin lives in Yaoundé, Cameroon, loves to travel and enjoys playing football with friends.

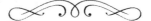

Jude A. Fonchenalla is a poet, editor, teacher and social worker. His poems have appeared in *Ashes and Memories* (2019, Editions Teham) and his writing focuses on issues related to leadership, youth and women's empowerment. His advocacy on gender and female reproductive rights is carried out under the auspices of the nonprofit, Vision In Action (VIAC). Jude is also co-founder of Zebra Comics, a leading comic

startup in Cameroon and has served the Afrikan Youth Movement as its editor-in-chief. He holds a BA in English Modern Letters (University of Yaoundé I), postgraduate diplomas from the Higher Teachers' Training College (Higher ENS), Yaoundé and the Humphrey School of Public Affairs, University of Minnesota.

M.D. Mbutoh is an award-winning poet from the North West Region of Cameroon. His literary works (poetry and short stories) have appeared in journals, blogs, and newspapers across the world including *Refugee Republic* (2017) and *Praxis*, (2017) a Nigerian literary magazine. His debut play, *Coastland of Hope* (2016) was commended by the BBC Radio Play in 2017. His works include: *Dance of the Kangaroos* (2018), and *Ashes and Memories* (2019). He has twice been guest writer in the Short Story Day Africa workshop and the Bakwa Creative Writing Workshop at the Goethe Institute, Yaounde respectively. Mbutoh holds a BA in English Language and Literature from the University of Yaoundé, Cameroon.

Spears Media Press LLC is an independent publisher dedicated to providing innovative publication strategies with emphasis on African/Africana stories and perspectives. As a platform for alternative voices, we prioritize the accessibility and affordability of our titles in order to ensure that relevant and often marginal voices are represented at the global marketplace of ideas. Our titles – poetry, fiction, narrative nonfiction, memoirs, reference, travel writing, African languages, and young people's literature – aim to bring African worldviews closer to diverse readers. Our titles are distributed in paperback and electronic formats globally by African Books Collective.

Visit us at www.spearsmedia.com

Printed in the United States
By Bookmasters